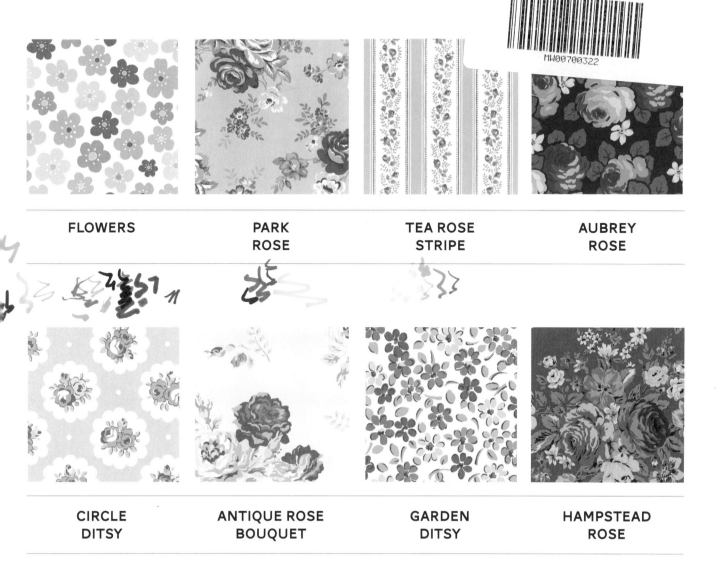

FLOWERS	**PARK ROSE**	**TEA ROSE STRIPE**	**AUBREY ROSE**

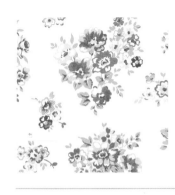   

CIRCLE DITSY	**ANTIQUE ROSE BOUQUET**	**GARDEN DITSY**	**HAMPSTEAD ROSE**

CRANHAM	**KEMPTON ROSE**	**KENTISH ROSE**	**KING STREET ROSE**

CAMDEN

**CHELSEA
FLOWERS**

**PAINTERLY
ROSE**

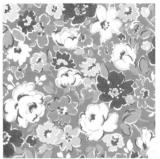

**MEWS
DITSY**

**ROSE
SPRIG**

**SPITALFIELDS
ROSE**

**HIGHBURY
ROSE**

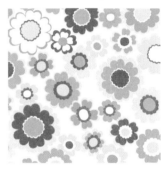

**ELECTRIC
FLOWERS**

**DAISY
BOUQUET**

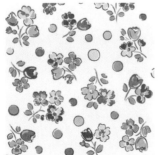

**SPOT
FLOWERS**

**SPRING
BOUQUET**

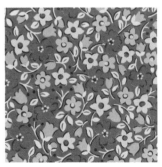

**PAINSWICK
DITSY**

| WINDSOR ROSE | GROVE ROSE | DAISY SPRAY | CUT ROSES |

| BUTTON ROSE | GARDEN ROSE | VICTORIA ROSE | KINGSWOOD ROSE |

| FRESTON ROSE | LITTLE LEAVES | HAMPTON ROSE | PAINTED ROSE |

INTRODUCTION

Inspired by growing up in the British countryside and a love of vintage prints, Cath Kidston opened her first shop in West London in 1993. More than 20 years later, our design team still takes inspiration from quirky vintage finds, creating colourful, modern vintage prints to brighten up your day. Our beautifully-detailed prints are designed in-house based on different themes and ideas and often include a nod to our British roots.

The Cath Kidston Floral Colouring Book brings together a collection of 43 much-loved, floral designs from the Cath Kidston archive that have been carefully recreated for you to colour in. Reimagine your old favourites and create some new ones, from classic large scale rosy prints to delicate ditsy florals. We've even included a handy Print Library showing all the prints in their original colourways.

Colouring the *The Cath Kidston Floral Colouring Book* will help to calm, relax and inspire you. Immerse yourself in the world of Cath Kidston prints and make our designs your own – it's the perfect outlet for your natural creativity.

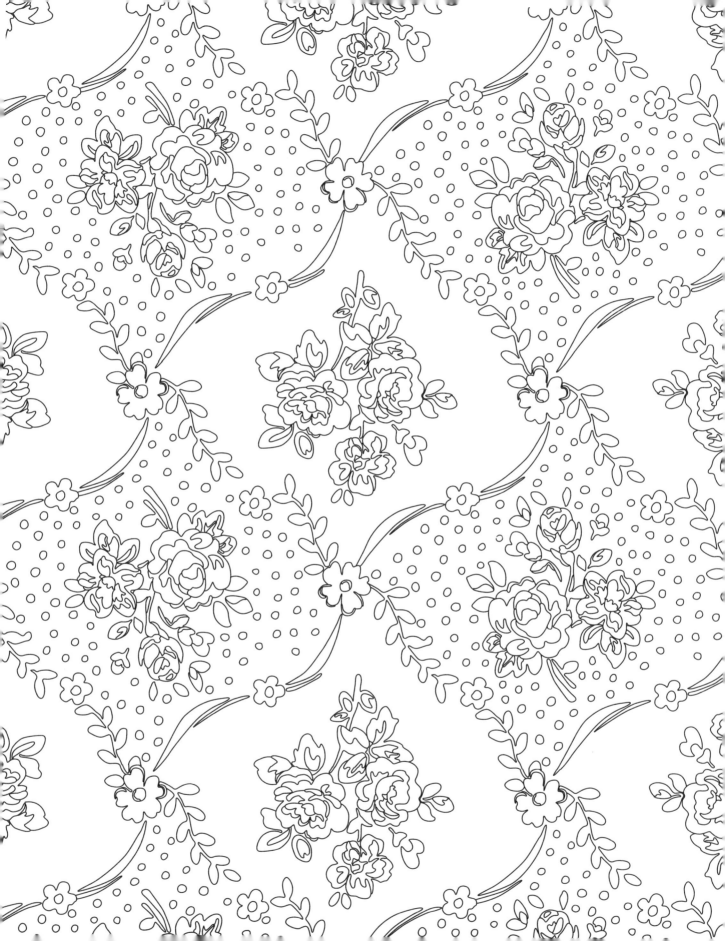

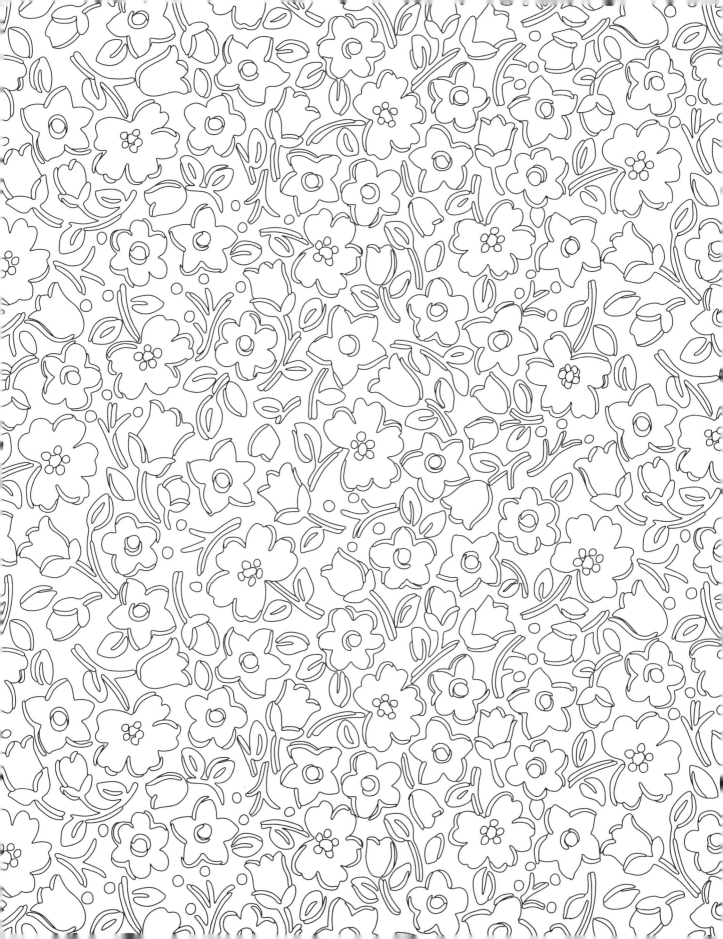